How to Eat Fried Worms

PICTURES BY EMILY McCULLY

How to Eat
Fried
Worms

THOMAS ROCKWELL

FRANKLIN WATTS | NEW YORK | LONDON

Library of Congress Cataloging in Publication Data

Rockwell, Thomas, 1933–
   How to eat fried worms.

   SUMMARY: Two boys set out to prove that worms can
make a delicious meal.
   [1. Humorous stories]   I. McCully, Emily Arnold,
illus.   II. Title.
PZ7.R5949Ho   [Fic]   73-4262
ISBN 0-531-02631-0

45 44 43 42 41
Design by Diana Hrisinko

7-15-00 B,T 21.25

I

II

III

IV

V

VI

VII

VIII

IX

X

XI

XII

XIII

XIV

Contents

The Bet   1

Digging   6

Training Camp   10

The First Worm   14

The Gathering Storm   22

The Second Worm   24

Red Crash Helmets and White Jump Suits   27

The Third Worm   30

The Plotters   33

The Fourth Worm   34

Tom   42

The Fifth Worm   46

Nothing to Worry About   48

The Pain and the Blood and the Gore   50

XV

XVI

XVII

XVIII

XIX

XX

XXI

XXII

XXIII

XXIV

XXV

XXVI

XXVII

XXVIII

XXIX

XXX

XXXI

XXXII

XXXIII

XXXIV

3:15 A. M. 54

The Sixth Worm 60

The Seventh Worm 61

The Eighth Worm 62

The Ninth Worm 63

Billy's Mother 68

The Tenth Worm 74

The Eleventh Worm 77

*Admirals Nagumo and Kusaka on the Bridge of
the* Akaiga, *December 6, 1941 78*

The Twelfth Worm 80

Pearl Harbor 82

Guadalcanal 83

The Thirteenth Worm 86

Hello, We're 90

92

The Peace Treaty 96

The Letter 98

Croak 101

The Fourteenth Worm 102

The Fifteenth 103

XXXV
XXXVI
XXXVII
XXXVIII
XXXIX

XL
XLI

Burp   105

The Fifteenth Wo   107

Out of the Frying Pan into the Oven   109

*$ % # ! Blip * + &!   111*

*The United States Cavalry Rides
    over the Hilltop   112*

The Fifteenth Worm   113

Epilogue   116

I

The Bet

HEY, *Tom!* Where were you last night?"

"Yeah, you missed it."

Alan and Billy came up the front walk. Tom was sitting on his porch steps, bouncing a tennis ball.

"Old Man Tator caught Joe as we were climbing through the fence, so we all had to go back, and he made us pile the peaches on his kitchen table, and then he called our mothers."

"Joe's mother hasn't let him out yet."

"Where were you?"

Tom stopped bouncing the tennis ball. He was a tall, skinny boy who took his troubles very seriously.

"My mother kept me in."

"What for?"

"I wouldn't eat my dinner."

Alan sat down on the step below Tom and began to chew his thumbnail.

"What was it?"

1

"Salmon casserole."

Billy flopped down on the grass, chunky, snub-nosed, freckled.

"Salmon casserole's not so bad."

"Wouldn't she let you just eat two bites?" asked Alan. "Sometimes my mother says, well, all right, if I'll just eat two bites."

"I wouldn't eat even one."

"That's stupid," said Billy. "One bite can't hurt you. I'd eat one bite of anything before I'd let them send me up to my room right after supper."

Tom shrugged.

"How about mud?" Alan asked Billy. "You wouldn't eat a bite of mud."

Alan argued a lot, small, knobby-kneed, nervous, gnawing at his thumbnail, his face smudged, his red hair mussed, shirttail hanging out, shoelaces untied.

"Sure, I would," Billy said. "Mud. What's mud? Just dirt with a little water in it. My father says everyone eats a pound of dirt every year anyway."

"How about poison?"

"That's different." Billy rolled over on his back.

"Is your mother going to make you eat the leftovers today at lunch?" he asked Tom.

"She never has before."

"How about worms?" Alan asked Billy.

Tom's sister's cat squirmed out from under the porch and rubbed against Billy's knee.

"Sure," said Billy. "Why not? Worms are just dirt."

"Yeah, but they bleed."

"So you'd have to cook them. Cows bleed."

"I bet a hundred dollars you wouldn't really eat a worm. You talk big now, but you wouldn't if you were sitting at the dinner table with a worm on your plate."

"I bet I would. I'd eat *fifteen* worms if somebody'd bet me a hundred dollars."

"You really want to bet? *I'll* bet you fifty dollars you can't eat fifteen worms. I really will."

"Where're you going to get fifty dollars?"

"In my savings account. I've got one hundred and thirty dollars and seventy-nine cents in my savings account. I know, because last week I put in the five dollars my grandmother gave me for my birthday."

"Your mother wouldn't let you take it out."

"She would if I lost the bet. She'd have to. I'd tell her I was going to sell my stamp collection otherwise. And I bought that with all my own money that I earned mowing lawns, so I can do whatever I want with it. I'll bet you fifty dollars you can't eat fifteen worms. Come on. You're chicken. You know you can't do it."

"*I* wouldn't do it," said Tom. "If salmon casserole makes me sick, think what fifteen worms would do."

Joe came scuffing up the walk and flopped down

beside Billy. He was a small boy, with dark hair and a long nose and big brown eyes.

"What's going on?"

"Come on," said Alan to Billy. "Tom can be your second and Joe'll be mine, just like in a duel. You think it's so easy—here's your chance to make fifty bucks."

Billy dangled a leaf in front of the cat, but the cat just rubbed against his knee, purring.

"What kind of worms?"

"Regular worms."

"Not those big green ones that get on the tomatoes. I won't eat those. And I won't eat them all at once. It might make me sick. One worm a day for fifteen days."

"And he can eat them any way he wants," said Tom. "Boiled, stewed, fried, fricasseed."

"Yeah, but we provide the worms," said Joe. "And there have to be witnesses present when he eats them; either me or Alan or somebody we can trust. Not just you and Billy."

"Okay?" Alan said to Billy.

Billy scratched the cat's ears. Fifty dollars. That was a lot of money. How bad could a worm taste? He'd eaten fried liver, salmon loaf, mushrooms, tongue, pig's feet. Other kids' parents were always nagging them to eat, eat; his had begun to worry about *how much* he ate. Not that he was *fat*. He just hadn't worked off all his winter blubber yet.

He slid his hand into his shirt and furtively squeezed the side of his stomach. Worms were just dirt; dirt wasn't fattening.

If he won fifty dollars, he could buy that minibike George Cunningham's brother had promised to sell him in September before he went away to college. Heck, he could gag *anything* down for fifty dollars, couldn't he?

He looked up. "I can use ketchup or mustard or anything like that? As much as I want?"

Alan nodded. "Okay?"

Billy stood up.

"Okay."

II

No," said Tom. "That's not fair."

He and Alan and Joe were wandering around behind the barns at Billy's house, arguing over where to dig the first worm.

"What d'ya mean, it's not fair?" said Joe. "Nobody said anything about where the worms were supposed to come from. We can get them anywhere we want."

"Not from a manure pile," said Tom. "That's not fair. Even if we didn't make a rule about something, you still have to be fair."

"What difference does it make where the worm comes from?" said Alan. "A worm's a worm."

"There's nothing wrong with manure," said Joe. "It comes from cows, just like milk." Joe was sly, devious, a schemer. The manure pile had been his idea.

"You and Billy have got to be fair, too," said Alan to Tom. "Besides, we'll dig in the old part of the pile, where it doesn't smell much anymore."

Digging

"Come on," said Tom, starting off across the field dragging his shovel. "If it was fair, you wouldn't be so anxious about it. Would you eat a worm from a manure pile?"

Joe and Alan ran to catch up.

"I wouldn't eat a worm, period," said Joe. "So you can't go by that."

"Yeah, but if your mother told you to go out and pick some daisies for the supper table, would you pick the daisies off a manure pile?"

"My mother wouldn't ask me. She'd ask my sister."

"You know what I mean."

Alan and Tom and Joe leaned on their shovels under a tree in the apple orchard, watching the worms they had dug squirming on a flat rock.

"Not him," said Tom, pointing to a night crawler.

"Why not?"

"Look at him. He'd choke a dog."

"*Geez!*" exploded Alan. "You expect us to pick one Billy can just *gulp* down, like an ant or a nit?"

"Gulping's not eating," said Joe. "The worm's got to be big enough so Billy has to cut it into bites and eat it with a fork. Off a plate."

"It's this one or nothing," said Alan, picking up the night crawler.

Tom considered the matter. It *would* be more fun watching Billy trying to eat the night crawler. He grinned. Boy, it was *huge!* A regular *python.* Wait till Billy saw it.

"We let you choose where to dig," said Alan.

After all, thought Tom, Billy couldn't expect to win fifty dollars by just gulping down a few measly little *baby* worms.

"All right. Come on." He turned and started back toward the barns, dragging his shovel.

III

S IX, seven, eight, nine, *ten!*"

Billy was doing push-ups in the deserted horse barn. He wasn't *worried* about eating the first worm. But people were always daring him to do things, and he'd found it was better to look ahead, to try to figure things out, get himself ready. Last winter Alan had dared him to sleep out all night in the igloo they'd built in Tom's backyard. Why not? Billy had thought to himself. What could happen? About midnight, huddled shivering under his blankets in the darkness, he'd begun to wonder if he should give up and go home. His feet felt like aching stones in his boots; even his tongue, inside his mouth, was cold. But half an hour later, as he was stubbornly dancing about outside in the moonlight to warm himself, Tom's dog Martha had come along with six other dogs, all in a pack, and Billy had coaxed them into the igloo and blocked the door with an orange crate, and after the dogs had stopped wrestling and nipping and barking and sniffing

Training Camp

around, they'd all gone to sleep in a heap with Billy in the middle, as warm as an onion in a stew.

But he hadn't been able to think of anything special to do to prepare himself for eating a worm, so he was just limbering up in general—push-ups, knee bends, jumping jacks—red-faced, perspiring.

Nearby, on an orange crate, he'd set out bottles of ketchup and Worchestershire sauce, jars of piccalilli and mustard, a box of crackers, salt and pepper shakers, a lemon, a slice of cheese, his mother's tin cinnamon-and-sugar shaker, a box of Kleenex, a jar of maraschino cherries, some horseradish, and a plastic honey bear.

Tom's head appeared around the door.

"Ready?"

Billy scrambled up, brushing back his hair.

"Yeah."

"TA RAHHHHHHHHH!"

Tom flung the door open; Alan marched in carrying a covered silver platter in both hands, Joe

slouching along beside him with a napkin over one arm, nodding and smiling obsequiously. Tom dragged another orange crate over beside the first; Alan set the silver platter on it.

"A chair," cried Alan. "A chair for the monshure!"

"Come on," said Billy. "Cut the clowning."

Tom found an old milking stool in one of the horse stalls. Joe dusted it off with his napkin, showing his teeth, and then ushered Billy onto it.

"Luddies and gintlemin!" shouted Alan. "I prezint my musterpiece: Vurm a la Mud!"

He swept the cover off the platter.

"Awrgh!" cried Billy, recoiling.

IV

THE huge night crawler sprawled limply in the center of the platter, brown and steaming.

"Boiled," said Tom. "We boiled it."

Billy stormed about the barn, kicking barrels and posts, arguing. "A night crawler isn't a *worm!* If it was a worm, it'd be called a worm. A night crawler's a night crawler."

Finally Joe ran off to get his father's dictionary:

night crawler n: EARTHWORM; esp: a large earthworm found on the soil surface at night

Billy kicked a barrel. It still wasn't fair; he didn't care what any dictionary said; everybody knew the difference between a night crawler and a worm—look at the thing. Yergh! It was as big as a souvenir pencil from the Empire State Building! Yugh! He poked it with his finger.

The First Worm

Alan said they'd agreed right at the start that he and Joe could choose the worms. If Billy was going to cheat, the bet was off. He got up and started for the door. He guessed he had other things to do besides argue all day with a fink.

So Tom took Billy aside into a horse stall and put his arm around Billy's shoulders and talked to him about George Cunningham's brother's minibike, and how they could ride it on the trail under the power lines behind Odell's farm, up and down the hills, bounding over rocks, rhum-rhum. Sure, it was a big worm, but it'd only be a couple more bites. Did he want to lose a minibike over *two bites?* Slop enough mustard and ketchup and horseradish on it and he wouldn't even taste it.

"Yeah," said Billy. "I could probably eat this one. But I got to eat *fifteen.*"

"You can't quit now," said Tom. "Look at them." He nodded at Alan and Joe, waiting beside the orange crates. "They'll tell everybody you were chicken. It'll be all over school. Come on."

He led Billy back to the orange crates, sat him down, tied the napkin around his neck.

Alan flourished the knife and fork.

"Would monshure like eet carved lingthvise or crussvise?"

"Kitchip?" asked Joe, showing his teeth.

"Cut it out," said Tom. "Here." He glopped ketchup and mustard and horseradish on the night crawler, squeezed on a few drops of lemon juice, and salted and peppered it.

Billy closed his eyes and opened his mouth. "Ou woot in."

Tom sliced off the end of the night crawler and forked it up. But just as he was about to poke it into Billy's open mouth, Billy closed his mouth and opened his eyes.

"No, let me do it."

Tom handed him the fork. Billy gazed at the dripping ketchup and mustard, thinking, Awrgh! It's all right talking about eating worms, but *doing* it!?!

Tom whispered in his ear. "Minibike."

"Glug." Billy poked the fork into his mouth, chewed furiously, *gulped!* . . . *gulped!* . . . His eyes crossed, swam, squinched shut. He flapped his arms wildly. And then, opening his eyes, he grinned beatifically up at Tom.

16

"Superb, Gaston."

Tom cut another piece, ketchuped, mustarded, salted, peppered, horseradished, and lemoned it, and handed the fork to Billy. Billy slugged it down, smacking his lips. And so they proceeded, now sprinkling on cinnamon and sugar or a bit of cheese, some cracker crumbs or Worcestershire sauce, until there was nothing on the plate but a few stray dabs of ketchup and mustard.

"Vell," said Billy, standing up and wiping his mouth with his napkin. "So. Ve are done mit de first curse. Naw seconds?"

"Lemme look in your mouth," said Alan.

"Yeah," said Joe. "See if he swallowed it all."

"Soitinly, soitinly," said Billy. "Luke as long as you vant."

Alan and Joe scrutinized the inside of his mouth.

"Okay, okay," said Tom. "Leave him alone now. Come on. One down, fourteen to go."

"How'd it taste?" asked Alan

"Gute, gute," said Billy. "Ver'fine, ver'fine. Hoo hoo." He flapped his arms like a big bird and began to hop around the barn, crying, "Gute, gute. Ver'fine, ver'fine. Gute, gute."

Alan and Joe and Tom looked worried.

"Uh, yeah—gute, gute. How you feeling, Billy?" Tom asked.

"Yeah, stop flapping around and come tell us how you're feeling," said Joe.

They huddled together by the orange crates as Billy hopped around and around them, flapping his arms.

"Gute, gute. Ver'fine, ver'fine. Hoo hoo."

Alan whispered, "He's crackers."

Joe edged toward the door. "Don't let him see we're afraid. Crazy people are like dogs. If they see you're afraid, they'll attack."

"It couldn't *be,*" whispered Tom, standing his ground. "One worm?"

"Gute, gute," screeched Billy, hopping higher and higher and drooling from the mouth.

"Come *on,*" whispered Joe to Tom.

"Hey, *Billy!*" burst out Tom suddenly in a hearty, quavering voice. "Cut it out, will you? I want to ask you something."

Billy's arms flapped slower. He tiptoed menacingly around Tom, his head cocked on one side, his cheeks puffed out. Tom hugged himself, chuckling nervously.

"Heh, heh. Cut it out, will you, Billy? Heh, heh."

Billy pounced. Joe and Alan fled, the barn door banging behind them. Billy rolled on the floor, helpless with laughter.

Tom clambered up, brushing himself off.

"Did you see their *faces?*" Billy said, laughing. "Climbing over each other out the door? Oh! Geez! Joe was pale as an onion."

"Yeah," said Tom. "Ha, ha. You fooled them."

"Ho! Geez!" Billy sat up. Then he crawled over to the door and peered out through a knothole. "Look at them, peeking up over the stone wall. Watch this."

The door swung slowly open.

Screeching, Billy hopped onto the doorsill!—into the yard!—up onto a stump!—splash into a puddle!—flapping his arms, rolling his head.

Alan and Joe galloped up the hill through the high grass, yelling, "Here he comes! Get out of the way!"

And then Billy stopped hopping, and climbing up on the stump, called in a shrill, girlish voice, "Oh, boy-oys, where are you go-ing? Id somefing tare you, iddle boys?"

Alan and Joe stopped and looked back.

"Id oo doughing home, iddle boys?" yelled Billy. "Id oo tared?"

"Who's scared, you lunk?" called Alan.

"Yeah," yelled Joe. "I guess I can go home without being called scared, if I want to."

"But ain't oo in a dawful hur-ry?" shouted Billy.

"I just remembered I was supposed to help my mother wash windows this afternoon," said Alan. "That's all." He turned and started up through the meadow, his hands in his pockets.

"Yeah," said Joe. "Me, too." He trudged after Alan.

21

V

ALAN and Joe stopped in the orchard by the pile of fresh dirt.

"You think he'll be able to do it?" asked Alan, biting his thumbnail.

"I don't know," said Joe.

"He can't do it," said Alan. "How could anybody eat fifteen worms? My father'll kill me. *Fifty dollars?* He ate that one awful easy."

"Forget it," said Joe. "If he doesn't give up himself, I'll figure something out. We could spike the next worm with pepper. He'd eat one piece and then another, talking to Tom—Then all of a sudden he'd sneeze: ka-chum! Then he'd sneeze again: ka-*chum!* Then again: ka-chum ka-chum! A faint look of panic would creep over his face; he's beginning to wonder if he'll ever stop. He clutches his stomach; his eyes begin to water. Ka-chum! Ka-chum!"

The Gathering Storm

"Billy's awful stubborn," said Alan. "Even if it was killing him, he might not give up."

"Ka-*chum!* Ka-*chum!*" cried Joe. "He falls to the floor. I bend over him. 'Gawd,' I say. 'Call his mother. It's the troglodycrosis.' His eyes bleat up at me. Ka-*chum!*"

"Remember that business last summer?" said Alan, gnawing on his thumbnail. "When it was ninety-five degrees in the shade and I dared him to put on all his winter clothes and his father's raccoon coat and his ski boots and walk up and down Main Street all afternoon?"

"Ka-*chum!* Ka-*chum!*"

They went off through the orchard, Joe sneezing, sighing, rolling his eyes—pretending to be Billy suffering from a dose of peppered worm; Alan moaning to himself about how stubborn Billy could be—*fifty dollars?*

VI

BILLY sighed. On the plate before him lay the last bite of worm under a daub of ketchup and mustard.

"What's the matter?" asked Tom.

"I don't know," sighed Billy. He picked up the fork again.

"Does it taste bad?"

"No," said Billy wearily. "I just taste ketchup and mustard mostly. But it makes me feel sort of sick. Even *before* I eat it. Just thinking about it." He sighed again and then glanced at Joe and Alan, talking to each other in whispers over by the window.

"What are you whispering about?"

"Nothing."

"Then what are you whispering for?"

The Second Worm

"Nothing. It's not important. Just something Joe's father told him last night."

"What?"

"Come on. Finish up. It was nothing. We'll miss the cartoons."

Billy shut his eyes and popped the last piece of worm into his mouth, chewed, gagged, clapped his hands over his mouth, *gulped! gulped!* toppled backward off the orange crate. Sprawling on his back in the chaff, he gazed peacefully up at the ceiling.

Joe and Alan stood over him.

"Open up."

Billy opened his mouth.

"Wider. See any, Joe?"

"Naw, he swallowed it."

"Okay, let's go."

Red Crash
Helmets and
White Jump Suits

AFTER the movies, Tom walked home with
Billy.

"Tomorrow I'll roll the crawler in cornmeal and
fry it. Like a trout."

"It's not really the taste," said Billy. "It's more
the thought. When I start to eat it, even though it's
smothered in ketchup and mustard and grated
cheese, I can't stop *thinking* worm. Worm, worm,
worm, worm, worm, worm: gaggles of worms in bait
boxes, drowned worms drying up on sidewalks, a
worm squirming as the fishhook gores into him, the
soggy end of a worm draggling out of a dead fish's
mouth, robins yanking worms out of a lawn. I can't
stop thinking worm."

"Yeah, but if I fry it in cornmeal, it won't *look*
like a crawler," said Tom. "I'll put parsley around
it, and some slices of lemon. And then you can con-
centrate, think fish. All the time you're waiting in
the barn, all the time you're eating it, keep saying to

yourself: fish fish fish fish fish fish fish fish; here I am
eating fish, good fish.

"Trout, salmon, flounder, perch,
I'll ride my minibike into church.
Dace, tuna, haddock, trout,
Wait'll you hear the minister shout.

"Fish fish fish fish fish fish fish fish fish fish fish fish
fish fish.

"Shark, haddock, sucker, eel,
I'll race my father in his automobile.
Eel, flounder, bluegill, shark,
We'll race all day till after dark."

Billy cheered up.
"Think how they'd all stare. I'd rev up the aisle,
zip around the front pews, down a side aisle under
the stained-glass windows. My parents would kill
me. Reverend Yarder'd peer down over the bible
stand. 'William,' he'd cry. 'William, you take that
engine thing out of here this minute!' "
"Yeah, and then they'd come chasing out after
us," said Tom.
Billy laughed. "Waving their arms and yelling.
And we'd lead them zigzag round and round and in
and out among the gravestones and monuments in
the cemetery and then roar off down the Sandgate

Road, leaving them draped over tombs, panting and shaking their fists."

"Hup hup!" yelled Tom, dancing around and boxing the air.

"And that Monday we'd smuggle it into class disguised as Raymond Dwelley, because he's so fat, and hide it in the coat closet. And then when Milly Butler said *anything*, anything at all, even something like 'excuse me,' or if she even sniffed, we'd dump a whole bottle of ink over her head and run for the coat closet, overturning chairs and desks behind us to slow up Mrs. Howard. She'd come after us, fuming and shouting threats, and suddenly the doors of the coat closet would slam open, and out we'd roar on our minibike in blood-red crash helmets and white jump suits, our scarves streaming out behind us! And we'd roar round and round the classroom while Mrs. Howard knelt among the overturned desks and chairs, sobbing helplessly into her hands, and then rhum-rhum out the door and up the hall, thumbing our noses at the monitors. Brackety-brackety-brackety up the stairs, stiff-arming tacklers, into Mr. Simmons's office—up onto his desk! *Broom! Broom!*—a backfire into his face, and *zoooom!* out the window as he topples backward in his chair in a hurricane of quiz papers and report cards. And then, crunch, landing on the driveway, we roar off down the highway to Bennington and join the Navy so Mrs. Howard and Mr. Simmons and our parents can't punish us."

VIII

TOM ran out of the kitchen of Billy's house, holding the sizzling frying pan out in front of him with both hands, the screen door banging behind him.

Alan threw open the barn door when he saw him coming. Tom thumped the frying pan down on the orange crate.

"There!" he said breathlessly. "Done to a T. Look at her, all golden-brown and sizzling. It looks good enough to eat."

"Yeah," said Billy. He poked the worm with his fork.

Tom took off the pot-holder glove he was wearing. "Think fish," he said. "Remember: think fish.

"Trout, salmon, flounder, perch,
    I'll ride my minibike into church.
    Eel, salmon, bluegill, trout,
    Wait'll you hear the minister shout.

"Clam, flounder, tuna, sucker,
    Look out here we come, old Mrs. Tucker.
    Lobster, black bass, oyster stew,
    There goes New Orleans, here comes Peru."

The Third Worm

He leaned over Billy and whispered in his ear,
"Fish fish fish fish fish fish fish fish fish, go on, take a
bite, fish fish fish fish fish, okay, second bite, fish,
fish, fish, fish. . . ."

IX

The Plotters

Geez, you think it'll work?" said Alan to Joe. "Suppose it doesn't? He didn't seem to pay much attention today."

"Don't worry," said Joe. "We got him thinking. It takes time. I got it all doped out. Trust me."

BILLY ate steadily, grimacing, rubbing his nose, spreading on more horseradish sauce. Tom bent over him, hissing in his ear, "Fish fish fish fish fish fish."

Billy paused, watching Alan and Joe whispering by the door. He swished the last bite round and round in the ketchup and mustard. All of a sudden he said, "That's not fair. They can't act like that anymore. Every time I swallow they lean forward as if they expected me to keel over or something! And then when I don't, they look surprised and shrug their shoulders and nudge each other."

"Come on," said Joe. "Cut it out. We can watch you, for cripes' sake. We're just standing over here by the window watching you."

"No, you're not," said Billy. "You're whispering. And acting as if you expected something to happen every time I swallow."

"It's nothing," said Joe. "Forget it. Look, we'll

The Fourth Worm

turn around and look out the window while you swallow."

"What do you mean, it's nothing?" said Billy. "What's nothing?"

"Oh, come on," said Alan. "It's just something Joe's father told him the other night. It's nothing."

"What? What?"

"It'll just worry you," said Alan. "It's crazy. It's nothing. Forget it."

Billy tore the napkin away from his throat.

"Tell me!"

"It's nothing," said Joe. "You know how my father is. He's always yelling about something."

"Tell me or it's all off."

"Well, look, it's nothing, but the night before last, I was telling Janie about you eating the worms and my father was on the porch and heard us. So he threw down his newspaper and says, 'Joseph!' So I

35

says, 'Yes, Pa?' And he says, 'Have you et a worm, Joseph?' And then he grabbed my shoulders and shook me till my hands danced at the ends of my arms like a puppet's. 'It's for your own good,' he says. So I stuttered out, 'It'ssss nnnnot going to ddddo me any ggggood if IIIII sssshake to ppppppieces, is it?' Janie was wailing; my mother was chewing her apron in the doorway. 'Alfred,' she cries, 'what's he done? You'll deracinate him. Has he hauled down the American flag at school and eaten it again? Has he —' "

"So what's the *point?*" yelled Billy. "Get to the *point!* What's it all have to do with *me?*"

"I'm coming to it," said Joe, wiping his nose. "But I wanted to show you how important it was, my father nearly killing me and all."

He sneezed. And then Alan began to sneeze and finally had to hobble off into one of the horse stalls, hugging his stomach, to recover.

"Anyway," said Joe, wiping his nose again and hitching up his Levi's, "so my father told my mother he thought I'd eaten a worm. 'A what?' says my mother, dropping her apron and clutching the sides of her head. 'A worm,' says my father, nodding solemnly. So my mother fainted, collapsed all helter-skelter right there in the doorway, and lay still, her tongue lolling out of her mouth, her red hair spread out beautifully over the doorsill. So I—"

"*Will you cut it out?*" Billy yelled. "Who cares

about your *mother? What does it have to do with ME?"*

"I think he's lying," said Tom. "Whoever heard of someone's mother fainting and her tongue hanging out?"

"All *RIGHT!"* yelled Joe apoplectically, stamping around. *"ALL RIGHT!* Now I *won't* tell. You can die, Billy Forrester, and *you'll* have to carry him home, Tom Grout, all by yourself! Nobody says to me: 'Who cares about your mother.' ALL RIGHT! I'm going. Alan," he yelled, "they're insulting my mother. I'm going."

"Don't," said Alan, running out of the horse stall and grabbing Joe by the shirttail. "Don't. You got to tell him. Even your mother'd say so. Mine, too. No matter what he said. Ain't it a matter of life and death?"

"I *won't,"* said Joe, starting toward the door.

Alan pulled him back. "You got to. How long have we known poor Bill? Six, seven years? For old time's sake, Joe, because we were all once in kindergarten together. Think of the agony he'll face, Joe, the pain and the blood and the gore."

Billy was on his knees by the orange crate, wringing his hands, not daring to interfere. But when Joe glanced sullenly back at him, he whispered, "Please, Joe? For old time's sake?"

"Well, will you apologize for insulting my mother?"

"I do," said Billy. "I do. I apologize."

So Alan and Joe began to sneeze again and this time had to bend over and put their heads between their legs to recover.

Tom, who had been watching them suspiciously,

trying to make out what was going on, started to say something. "Shut up!" hissed Billy fiercely, turning on him. "You keep out of it!"

So Joe went on with his story: how his mother had been carried upstairs to her room; how the doctor had come, shaking his head; how his aunt had sobbed, pulling down all the shades in their house; how that morning his mother had finally come downstairs for the first time leaning on his aunt's arm, pale and sorrowful; how . . .

"Yeah," said Tom. "Sure. So why? What does eating worms do to you?"

"Nobody will tell me," said Joe, opening his eyes wide. "It's been three days now, and nobody'll say. It's just like the time my cousin Lucy got caught in the back seat of her father's Cheverolet with the encyclopedia salesman. Nobody'll tell me why there was such an uproar." He wiped his mouth. "But one thing's sure: it's worse than poison. Probably—"

"Crap," said Tom.

"Oh, yeah?" said Joe.

But then he and Alan had another sneezing fit, sprawling helplessly against each other.

"Look at them," said Tom to Billy. "They're not sneezing—they're laughing. Come on. Eat the last piece and let's get out of here."

"You really think so?" said Billy doubtfully. The sneezing did look an awful lot like giggling.

"Sure. Look at them."

Tom gave Alan and Joe a shove. They collapsed in a heap, sneezing uncontrollably.

Billy watched them. Yeah, sure, they weren't sneezing—they were laughing. . . . Weren't they?

"Hay fever," gasped Alan, "hay fever."

"Aw, you never had hay fever before," said Tom. "How about yesterday or the day before? Come on, Billy. Open up."

So Billy, half believing Tom and half not, glancing doubtfully at Alan and Joe, allowed Tom to poke the last bite of worm into his mouth and lead him out of the barn.

Alan and Joe sat up.

"It didn't work," said Alan.

Joe began to brush the chaff out of his hair.

"You wait. He wasn't sure. Tom was, but *he* isn't eating the worms. You wait. Billy's worried. He was before, that's why he said he felt like he was going to throw up. But now he's *really* worried. Suppose I *wasn't* lying? Did you see his face when I said my father shook me? I thought his eyes would bug right out of his head."

Alan laughed. "Oh, geez, yeah. And when you said your mother fainted."

Joe stopped brushing the chaff out of his hair. "Except why'd you laugh so much, for cripes' sake? If you'd kept a straight face even Tom wouldn't have guessed."

"Aw, you laughed first. What do you mean?"

"Me? *I* laughed first? I did not."

"You did so. You laughed when he yelled at you the first time. You wiped your nose."

They went off through the meadow, arguing.

XI

BILLY pushed the frying pan toward Tom.

"Okay, fink. If it's not supposed to hurt you, *you* eat a piece."

"Oh, no," said Alan. He and Joe were lying on their stomachs in the hayloft, watching. "If he eats a piece, you lose, Billy. The bet was *you* were going to eat fifteen worms, not you and him together."

Billy didn't look up, his eyes fixed grimly on Tom.

"All right. Then I'll go dig *another* worm, just for him. He's so *big*, telling me: 'Hurry up, hurry up, I can't wait around all day—don't be a sissy.' All right. Now—"

"I didn't say sissy," said Tom uncomfortably. "I just said if the first four worms didn't kill you, this one wouldn't. I can't help it if my mother told me to be home by two today. She's going shopping, so I have to mind my brother."

Tom

"Yeah?" said Billy. "Okay. So we'll just have time for you to eat a worm before you go. Come on. Where's the shovel?"

"Here," said Alan from the loft. "We brung an extra today."

A worm dangled squirming from his fingers. He dropped it to Billy.

"It's not cooked," said Tom.

"I'll do it, I'll do it," said Joe, scrambling down the ladder. He took the worm from Billy and ran out, then ran back and grabbed the frying pan.

Tom sat down on an overturned pail to wait. He didn't want to eat any worm. It wasn't *his* bet. He glanced at the door creaking in the wind. Maybe he should make a break for it.

Of course, he could see Billy's point. Billy didn't believe Joe's story, but still . . . he'd find it reassuring if Tom ate some worm, too.

"He'll eat it," Billy was saying to Alan.

"If he don't, he's chicken," said Alan. "After all his talk."

Why *don't* I eat it? thought Tom. I mean, it's a yucky thing to do, but it wouldn't *kill* me.

He scratched his neck, shifting his seat on the pail.

I don't know, thought Tom. I just won't, I guess.

He gagged, imagining what it would be like to bite down on a soft, fat, boiled worm. He glanced at the door again.

Billy kicked the door shut.

"Leave it open," said Tom.

"Why?"

"Because I said so."

"Yeah? Well, you don't own this barn."

"Neither do you. Your father does."

Billy rubbed his nose, watching Tom, figuring: He's trying to pick a fight so he won't have to eat the worm.

"Okay."

Billy opened the door and set a brick against it.

Tom shifted his seat on the pail again. He couldn't stop thinking about what it would be like to bite down on a soft, fat, boiled worm. He scratched his ear. Who did Billy think he was, trying to order people around, telling them what they had to eat and all? Billy wasn't anybody's father. Tom began to feel put-upon and indignant and stubborn.

A screen door slammed: Joe coming back with the worm. Tom licked his lips. He heard Joe running across the barnyard toward them . . .

"Billy!" Alan shouted.

Billy spun around just in time to catch a glimpse of Tom pelting out the door, the door banging shut. He flung to the window: Joe sprawled in the middle of the barnyard on his back, Tom was clambering over the wall into the meadow, the frying pan lay upside down beside the horse trough.

XII

LOOK, said Billy to himself, staring down at the fried worm on the plate. Be sensible. How can it hurt me? I've eaten four already. Tom was just scared. He's like that. He eggs other people on, but he never wants to do anything himself.

"Give up?" asked Alan.

"Come on," said Joe. "We haven't got all day."

"Five more minutes," said Alan. "Then I win."

"There's no time limit," said Billy. For the first time he wondered what he'd do if he lost. Where could he ever get fifty dollars? But how could he eat *ten more?* Big, fat, ugly, soft, brown things. He couldn't ask his father for fifty dollars.

He heard Alan and Joe whispering together.

The Fifth Worm

"He's gonna quit."

"Yeah. I knew he'd never make it when I bet with him. He talks big. Him and Tom are just the same. But they never *do* anything."

Billy gritted his teeth, glopped on ketchup, mustard, salt, grated cheese, whatever was on the crate, anything, everything, and then grabbed up the worm and tore it apart with his hands, stuffing it into his mouth, chewing and chewing and swallowing, gulping. . . .

Then, panting, he reached out and wiped his gooey hands on Alan's trousers and grinned messily up at him and said,

"There. Five."

XIII

THAT night Alan asked his father to show him fifty dollars.

After that, he couldn't sleep, tossing and turning in his rumpled bed. Suppose he lost? He could just see himself asking his father for fifty dollars— *begging* for it, on his knees, tears streaming down his cheeks; and then, at Thanksgiving dinner, cringing while all his aunts and uncles and cousins roared over his father's story of "Alan's bet."

He slid out of bed and snuck down the carpeted hall to his parents' bedroom.

"You got to wake him, Mrs. O'Hara, you *got* to," he whispered into the phone. "It's an emergency. I *got* to speak to him." Pause. "I got a hoarse throat, Mrs. O'Hara, that's why I'm whispering. Please." Pause. "Gee, thanks, Mrs. O'Hara. No, I won't ever call this late again, it's just it's—"

He waited, gnawing at his thumbnail. A board creaked on the stairs. He stiffened. Silence.

"What d'ya *want?*" said Joe suddenly over the telephone. "Geez, I was *sleeping*. You woke me up."

Nothing to Worry About

"Joe, suppose I lose? My father'll *never* let me take the money out of my savings account. I know he won't. You think I'll lose, Joe? Huh? Huh? Joe, tell me. Give it to me straight. Joe, I got to know. I can't sleep."

Joe sighed. "Look. I told you this afternoon. You got nothing to worry about. He's cracking. Sure, he ate that one today. Sure, he might—"

XIV

Four blocks away Billy suddenly found himself in a brightly lit butcher shop, jostled by a crowd of enormous, pigeon-breasted, middle-aged women, shouting to make himself heard over the din of their chatter and the roars of butchers ordering about the weasel-faced boys who were lugging haunches and tubs of meat in and out of the refrigerator room in the rear. Then a butcher saw Billy jumping and jumping among the women and asked for his order and Billy gave it, and suddenly he was shoved up close to the chopping block and the butcher slapped down ten black worms as big as snakes and Billy tried to say they were too big, he'd choke on them, but the butcher couldn't hear him over the thumps of his cleaver and the din of the women and the hoarse shouts of the other butchers, and before Billy knew what was happening, he was seated at a table

The Pain and
the Blood
and the Gore

in Longchamps Restaurant on Times Square in New York City with a large napkin tied under his chin, and a waiter was uncovering a platter on which lay one of the huge black worms, coiled snakily, a red, red rose wobbling in the center of its coils.

"How can I ever finish it?" said Billy and cut into a mammoth coil. Steaming pink juice flooded out. Billy ate and ate and ate and ate and then looked . . . and . . . and . . . he *must* have eaten more than *that?* And then he looked again and there was no hole at all. He had eaten and eaten and eaten . . . nothing at all!

And then he felt something cold on his ankles and looked under the tablecloth and there were two more of the huge worms wound around and around his ankles. And then he felt something weighing down his arm and he looked and there was another worm wound around his arm, glaring hungrily at him with its bloodshoot eyes, and from everywhere in the vast room, winding between the tables, waiters approached carrying huge silver serving platters. . . .

Billy opened his eyes.

For the first moment, in the moonlight flooding his bedroom, his two bare feet, sticking up out of the bottom of the covers, looked like two huge white worms' heads.

And then he realized that he had been dreaming and sank back onto his pillow, the nightmare melting away. There were no huge worms as big as pythons, he was home in bed, his parents were asleep in the next room. . . .

His stomach rumbled.

But suppose Joe hadn't *been lying?*

The hair stood up on the back of his neck.

Or suppose Joe had *made it all up but had been right anyway, without knowing it?*

A shutter banged. Billy glanced out the window and saw the moon riding among the tossing leaves. His stomach rumbled and gurgled.

He groaned.

Suppose he was dying? He'd heard of people waking up in the middle of the night with pains in their stomachs, and then, as the windows turned gray in the dawn, they died. Toadstools, soured lobster, tainted pork.

That was a *pain!*

He clutched his stomach, and groaning, half fell, half staggered out of bed and hobbled toward the door, bent double. Maybe there was an antidote. He whimpered. It didn't hurt a lot, but nothing ever did to begin with, did it?

HIS mother reached out and switched on the light. "What kind of pain, Billy?"

He stood beside the bed, clutching his stomach. "In my stomach. Oooo, there it goes again, I think."

"Did you eat something before bed?"

She was pulling on her bathrobe. "John, John."

3:15 A.M.

She shook her husband's shoulder. He mumbled sleepily. "Did you eat candy or something before bed, Billy?"

"Worms," groaned Billy.

"*Worms?* John! John! Billy, what kind of worms?"

55

"Regular worms, night crawlers."

She felt his forehead, lifted his chin to look in his face. "You don't have a temperature. How many worms did you eat?"

"Five. Two boiled and three fried. With ketchup, mustard, horseradish, salt, pepper, butter. To make them taste better."

"Fried? Ketchup? Taste better? John! Wake up."

"I had this bet with Alan. Ohhhhh." He groaned again.

"Take your hands away. Where does it hurt now? Show me."

"It doesn't really hurt so much now. It's just rumbling and gurgling something awful. It's—"

"Then why are you groaning?" asked his father, sitting up.

"Because I'm afraid it's going to *start* hurting. Do you think I'm going to die, Daddy?"

"Worms?" his father asked. "Ordinary worms? Earthworms?"

Billy nodded.

"And how many did you eat this evening?"

"One this afternoon. I've eaten one every day for the last five days. But they weren't little ones; they were night crawlers, huge ones, as big as snakes almost."

His father lay back down, pulling the covers up

around his shoulders. "Don't worry. Eating one night crawler a day for *six weeks* wouldn't hurt you. Go back to bed. It's probably all the ketchup and mustard that's upsetting your stomach. Drink a glass of warm water."

"John, are you sure?" said Billy's mother. "It doesn't seem to me that worms could be a very healthy thing to eat. John?"

His father snuggled deeper under the covers. "I didn't say eating worms would turn him into an All-American fullback. I just said they wouldn't hurt him. Now let's go to sleep."

Billy's mother glanced at Billy, shivering beside the bed in bare feet and pajamas, and then shook her husband again. "John? John, wake up. I think you should call Dr. McGrath. You don't really know whether or not eating worms is harmful. I know you don't."

Billy's father groaned and sat up. "Now, look. I am not going to call Dr. McGrath at three thirty in the morning to ask if it's all right for my son to eat worms. That's flat. Secondly, I *do* know that Billy's not going to die before morning. If worms were poisonous, which they're not, he would have been laid up before this. Billy, you've been eating worms for five days?"

Billy nodded.

"All right. And thirdly, I ate a *live* crayfish when I was in college and have suffered no discernible ill effects. And fourthly: I am going to *sleep*."

Billy's mother slipped her feet into her slippers, stood up and buttoned her bathrobe, and then leaned over the bed and shook her husband's shoulder. "John? John, I won't be able to sleep until you call. John? John, what about tapeworms or a fungus? John? Wake up. Billy, you go back to bed. Your father will call Dr. McGrath. John? John?"

Billy lay in bed listening to his mother and father arguing in their bedroom. He could only make out a word here and there, usually when his father started to shout, only to be shushed immediately by his mother. Billy got sleepier and sleepier. His stomach had stopped rumbling and gurgling. It was warm and cozy under the covers after standing on the cold floor in his bare feet. Then, in the midst of a foggy drowse, he heard someone dialing the phone in the hall outside his parents' bedroom, and then his father say, "Poison Control?" and explain the case.

Then there was a silence. Billy heard the water running in the bathroom. And then his father said, "You're sure? These weren't little ones. These were nightcrawlers." Pause. "And no long-range ill effects?" Pause. His father laughed. "A bet, I think."

And the next thing Billy knew, sunlight was streaming through his window and Emily was skipping down the hall past his door singing,

"Half a pound of tupenny rice,
Half a pound of treacle,
That's the way the money goes—"

His father shouted down the stairs, "Helen, do you know where my green tie with the red stripes is?"

XVI
The Sixth Worm

BILLY gulped it triumphantly, serene, untroubled.

By the door Alan glowered, his mind racing: He's gonna do it, he'll win, what'll I do? Fifty dollars.

Joe sat on an overturned pail, whistling, gazing carelessly about . . . sneaking a glance now and then at Billy. What had gone wrong? Why hadn't he cracked?

Outside, Tom lurked sheepishly in the bushes behind the stone wall, peering at the barn.

XVII
The Seventh Worm

BILLY ate it offhand, sideways, reading a comic book.

Alan and Joe squatted glumly in the barn door, watching him.

As Billy was daubing horseradish sauce on the last bite, Tom's head appeared in a corner of the grimy window. He waved tentatively at Billy.

Ignoring him, Billy gulped down the last bite, wiped his mouth, and tucking his comic book under his arm, strolled airily out of the barn, remarking over his shoulder, "See you tomorrow, fellows."

XVIII

The Eighth Worm

W<small>HERE'S</small> Joe?" asked Billy, spreading mustard down the length of the fried worm.

"He wouldn't come," said Alan sullenly. "It's no fair putting on that much mustard."

"Ha, ha," said Billy. "Who says? I can put on as much as I like of whatever I like, and you know it. Why wouldn't he come?"

"How should I know?"

Billy swooshed a bit of worm around in ketchup and horseradish sauce. "I know why he didn't."

"Yeah. You're so smart. Big deal." Alan couldn't get the fifty dollars out of his head. What was his father going to say when he told him he'd bet fifty dollars and lost? Geez! He gnawed at his thumbnail.

"He wouldn't come because he knows I've won. He knows I could eat *twenty* worms if I had to."

"Yeah? Yeah? Well, you ain't won yet. There's still seven to go. You act so big. Wait'll you begin to feel it in your stomach. You think you know everything. Yeah. You'll see. You wait."

"Ha, ha," said Billy. "You think you can scare me talking like that? Phooey." He strolled past Alan out into the sunlight.

"Hi," said Tom, popping up from behind a barrel.

"Pfffffft!" said Billy disdainfully and walked on.

XIX

The Ninth Worm

THAT's not a *worm!*" yelled Billy. "How can it be a worm? Geez, it must be *two feet long!*"

"It's a worm," said Alan stubbornly. "It's just like all the others. I rolled it in cornmeal and fried it."

"It's over two feet long!" screeched Billy.

He knew something was up. Otherwise Joe wouldn't have come back, slouching in the doorway pretending to be gazing up at the clouds. But Billy noticed he kept glancing at Alan and him. And Tom was peering in the window again. Something was up.

"Look," said Alan. "I'll cut it. You can see for yourself it's a worm. There. See? Come on. Eat up. We ain't got all day. Joe and me have to go to Shushan with his father."

Billy poked at the huge worm with his fork. Something sure was up. He ate the piece Alan had cut, looking the rest of the worm over carefully as he chewed. He ate another bite. Fauh! He'd forgotten to dip it in the horseradish sauce.

"Come on, come on, come on," said Alan.

"Yeah," said Joe. "Eat up, Billy, we got to go."

I'll never be able to eat the whole thing, thought Billy. It'd choke me; it's too much yuck at once.

"Half," he croaked. "I'll eat half. This is some

sort of a ringer. There's never *been* a worm this long."

"Okay," said Alan. "Then the bet's off. Suit yourself. Come on, Joe, he chickened out. Let's go."

"All right, all right," said Billy, playing for time. "The whole thing."

"You'll make yourself sick," said Alan.

He's too anxious, thought Billy. What's going on?

"Leave him alone," said Joe. "Let him eat it. It's *his* stomach."

He's trying to cover for Alan, thought Billy. He ate another bite. Then he began to scrape the cornmeal carefully off the worm with his knife.

"What are you doing?" said Alan.

"I think I'll have it *plain* today. No cornmeal."

"That's not *fair!* You can't—"

"*Glue!*" screamed Billy all of a sudden. "Glue! You glued two crawlers *together! Geez!* You bunch of lousy *cheats!* Tom! Tom, look what they tried to pull! *Glue!*"

Panting, Tom bent over the plate. "You're right. Geez!"

Alan kicked a pail clattering against the wall. "I told you it wouldn't work!" he screamed at Joe.

"All right. So it didn't work. You couldn't think of anything better."

"That's *cheating!*" said Billy. "I ought to win right now. You cheated."

"Fifteen worms in fifteen days!" yelled Joe. "You ain't won yet!"

"But you *cheated!*" shouted Tom.

"So *what?*"

They argued and yelled, striding here and there

about the barn, sprawling against posts, flinging up their arms, kicking walls, banging down on a pail or orange crate and squeezing their heads between their hands.

"It doesn't make any *difference!*" Joe yelled at Billy. "It didn't *work!* You didn't *fall for it!* If you'd eaten the whole thing and *then* found out it was two worms glued together, *then* you could have claimed to win because Alan was cheating."

"Big mouth!" shouted Alan from the horse stall, where he was kicking the slats in. "Who thought it up? Not me!"

"Who cares who thought it up?" shouted Tom. "It's still cheating!"

A pig looked in at the door and then wandered away.

Joe ran out and stuck his head under the faucet by the kitchen steps. A minute later he came running back dripping, yelling, "That's not *true!*"

"What's not true?" said Billy, turning around from shouting at Alan.

"Whatever you said."

"What'd I say?"

"It doesn't make any difference. You're a liar and a cheat and so *anything* you say isn't true."

"You're crazy. Even Hitler or—or Jack the Ripper—sometimes said things that were true. It's *impossible* to lie all the time."

Behind them Tom lay down on his back and said, "Arrgh!"

Alan and Joe and Billy turned to look at him.

"What's the matter with you?"

"ARRRGH!"

"Argh?"

"ARRRGH!"

Silence. A bird flew in and then out through a broken window in the loft.

"Well," said Billy. "Yeah. I see what you mean."

He and Alan and Joe sat down on the overturned orange crates. After a while Joe said, "Anyway, I was right. If Billy'd eaten it, it would have been cheating. But he didn't, so it's not. The bet's still on."

The pig looked in at the door again.

"A pig's loose," said Alan. "Look."

"Where?" said Billy. "Oh boy, come on. We gotta catch it." He jumped up. The pig bolted.

"Whooooeeeeee!" yelled Billy, dashing out. Tom and Joe and Alan scrambled after him.

BILLY slumped at the kitchen table on one elbow, pawing in his bowl of Wheaties with his spoon. His mother was washing the breakfast dishes at the sink.

"But *why* isn't it good to eat hot dogs for breakfast? I know nobody *does*. But why *don't* they?"

"Oh, *Billy,*" said his mother. "Stop it. Finish your cereal."

"Well, but—"

A knock on the screen door.

Billy's mother glanced around. "Oh, hello, Alan, Joe. Is your sister better, Joe?"

"Yes, thank you."

"Billy can't come out until he's finished his breakfast. Would you like to wait for him on the front porch?"

"We came to see you, Mrs. Forrester."

"Oh? Come in."

Billy's Mother

"Mrs. Forrester," said Joe, as Alan shut the door carefully behind them. "I don't know if you know about it already, but see, about a week ago Alan made this bet with Billy about eating worms. If Billy could eat fifteen worms, one each day for fif teen days, then—"

"Billy! You're not still eating them?"

Billy stuffed a spoonful of Wheaties into his mouth.

"Not just worms, Mom. I been eating lots of other stuff, too. Look at me. I'm healthy. Dr. McGrath told you the worms wouldn't hurt me."

"But Billy, Dr. McGrath didn't think you were going to *keep on* eating worms."

Joe nudged Alan and grinned.

"Aw, Mom, if five worms wouldn't hurt me, a few more won't either. They're little worms. Besides, it's a bet. If I—"

"They're *big* worms, Mrs. Forrester," said Joe, looking virtuous. "We won't lie to you. My mother told me never to tell a lie."

"Manure," said Billy. "Mom, it's a bet. I told you. If I win, Alan's got to pay me fifty dollars."

"Fifty dollars! Young man, don't you move from that chair." She went off into the front hall.

"Finks!" whispered Billy. "But you'll see. It won't work."

Alan and Joe gazed nonchalantly at the ceiling.

Billy's mother's voice came from the front hall. "Dr. McGrath, I'm awfully sorry to bother you again, it's such a ridiculous matter, but since I spoke to you, Billy has continued to eat worms." Pause. "No, no, it's nothing like that. He's acting perfectly normal otherwise. It seems he's made a bet with some other boys." Pause. "One every day. He has to eat fifteen to win his bet." Pause. "Oh, thank you, Dr. McGrath. I'm so sorry to bother—"

She returned to the kitchen. "But no more bets after this one, Billy. Alan and Joe, don't you egg him on anymore. He's far too eager to do wild things."

Billy yukked silently at Joe and Alan. Alan made a rude gesture at him.

"Mrs. Forrester," said Joe, "what we really came about is that Alan and me are going up to Lake Lauderdale today with my father to fish. And we won't be back till tomorrow night, so we wondered if you'd make sure Billy eats the worms today and tomorrow. It's not that we don't trust Billy, Mrs. Forrester—"

"No," said Billy's mother, smiling.

"—but it's always better if there's a referee. You know, like Mr. Simmons says at school: to save arguments and hard feelings. We brought the two worms." He held up a paper bag. "We boiled them already, so you can just keep them in the refrigerator."

"Well," said Billy's mother. "This is quite a responsibility. Are you sure I'll be neutral enough? I *am* his mother."

"Yeah, we thought of that," said Joe, "but we figured, well, you're usually pretty fair, and besides, parents almost never cheat kids if it's just something between kids. They're usually pretty fair until *they* get into it."

Billy's mother laughed. "And how does he eat them? Just cold boiled?"

"Well, we been frying them, Mrs. Forrester. We roll them in cornmeal and then fry them like a fish. But he can do whatever he wants. Except that Alan and me have decided it's not fair to make soup out of them or chop them all up like hash or a chicken-salad sandwich. He's got to eat them piece by piece."

"Who said?" yelled Billy. "When was that ever in the rules?"

"*We* said!" shouted Alan.

Billy jumped up, kicking his chair over. "Well,
then I *win!* Because it's cheating to make up new
rules in the middle."

"Oh, yeah?" shouted Alan. "Then you *lose!* Because *anybody* knows it'd be cheating to hash it up."

"You think you're going to weasel out of it after I've already eaten *nine!*"

"Who's weaseling? You're *cheating!*"

"Yeah?"

"Yeah!"

"Boys! *Boys!* Billy! Alan!"

Silence.

"Please. Now Billy, I think—no, let me speak first. I do think Alan and Joe are right. It wouldn't be fair to cut the worm all up. You can just think of some other way of fixing it. Thank you, Joe."

She took the paper bag and looked inside. "Pew. Billy, are you sure—"

"Mom, you've eaten eels; you ate eels last summer in Long Island. These are just smaller. They're the same thing."

"Well." She put the paper bag in the refrigerator. "I guess if Dr. McGrath says it's all right. Now why don't you all go outside?"

"I wouldn't go across the street with those finks," said Billy. "They can—"

"Yeah?" shouted Alan. "Well, who'd want to go anywhere with you, either?"

"Yeah?" shouted Billy.

"*Boys!*" cried Mrs. Forrester. "Stop it! All right. Alan and Joe, you had better go."

The screen door banged behind them.

"*Pfffft!*" said Billy scornfully.

Joe's face appeared at the screen. "Thanks for saying you'll help out, Mrs. Forrester."

XXI

WHAT'S for dinner?" said Billy's father, coming into the kitchen.

"Well," said Billy's mother. "You and I and Emily are having hamburgers and string beans and mashed potatoes. Billy is having a fried worm."

"More worms? The bet's still on?"

"Look." She took a small plate covered with Saran Wrap out of the refrigerator.

"And you've eaten nine of these already, Billy?" He poked the worms curiously. "What do you do, use a lot of ketchup and mustard?"

Billy nodded. "And horseradish and other things. And we fry them."

Billy's father lifted a corner of the Saran Wrap and smelled the worms. "Helen, you ought to be able to do better than fried. Use your cookbooks."

"I'm not the cook. I'm just the referee."

"Oh, come on. Think of the challenge."

He took a cookbook from the shelf under the spice rack. "Let's see. *Mastering the Art of French Cooking.*" He leafed through the cookbook. "Here. How about Poached Eels on Toast?"

"No," said Billy's mother. "It calls for chopping up the eel in little pieces, and that would be against the rules."

"How about Spaghetti with Wormballs then? Or

74

The Tenth Worm

a Savory Worm Pie? Creamed Worms on Toast? Spanish Worm? Wormloaf with Mushroom Sauce?"

"Wait," said Billy's mother, putting down her cooking spoon. "It might just—" She took the cookbook and turned to the index. "Here." She read: "Alsatian Smothered Worm: dredge the worm with seasoned flour. Saute in three tablespoons drippings until browned. Cover with sliced onions, pour over one cup thick sour cream, cover pot closely, and bake in a slow oven until tender."

"Bravo," said Billy's father. "Put the hamburgers back in the refrigerator. We'll *all* have worm tonight."

"I won't," said Emily.

"Ha," said Billy, grinning in the midst of chewing. "Boy, Alan and Joe thought they were doing me in when they came to you, Mom, but this is better than steak. It really tastes *good*."

"Yug," muttered Emily, making a face.

"Let me have a taste," said Billy's father.

"No, no," said his mother. "Billy has to eat every bit himself. Alan and Joe were very firm about that, and I'm the referee."

"Boy," said Billy. "I don't mind if it tastes like this."

The Eleventh Worm

HOW'D you do it?" said Billy. "What's it called?"

"My word," said his father.

"Gosh, Mrs. Forrester," gasped Tom.

On a silver dish in front of Billy lay an ice-cream cake bathed in fruit syrups—peach, cherry, tutti-frutti, candied orange—topped with whipped cream sprinkled with jelly beans and almond slivers.

"It's called a Whizbang Worm Delight," said Billy's mother proudly. "I made it up."

"Is the worm really in there?" said Billy, poking about with his spoon. And then, scraping away a bit of whipped cream at one end, he glimpsed the worm's snout protruding from the center of the cake.

"Snug as a bug in a rug," said his mother.

"I still wouldn't eat a worm," said Emily, eyeing the Whizbang Worm Delight with envious distaste.

"I would," said Tom. "At least, maybe I would."

XXIII

IT won't work."

"Look," said Joe, "even if he remembers the worm while we're at Shea, he can't get one. Where's anyone going to find a worm at Shea Stadium? Don't *worry,* we'll say, you've won; we'll find a worm after we get home. And we keep right on stuffing him: peanuts, hot dogs, hamburgers, Cracker Jack, ice cream, orange soda, gum, Mars Bars. You know how he loves to eat. You ever seen him refuse something to eat? By the time we start home he'll be bloated, drowsy, belching. Remember the last time? When *his* father took us? He was asleep by the time we hit Peekskill. Your father'll carry him in from the car; *his* mother and father'll put him to bed; next morning he'll wake up—TOO LATE! *You've won!* Fifteen worms in fifteen days! He *missed* a day!"

Admirals Nagumo and Kusaka on the Bridge of the Akaiga, December 6, 1941

Alan gnawed at his thumbnail. "What about Tom?"

"We'll ask him along and then just not pick him up. We can tell your father and Billy that Tom's mother called, he was sick, his grandmother died, anything, just so we don't have to bring him with us."

Alan sighed. "Geez, it'll probably cost me eight dollars just to buy all that food—Cracker Jack, hamburgers—"

"Yeah, but it'll cost you *fifty* dollars if he wins."

"Yeah, well—oh Geez, how'd I ever get into this? If my father finds out—"

Alan slumped on the porch steps, gazing down at his sneakers, gnawing his thumbnail.

"Come on," said Joe, slapping him on the shoulder. "Cheer up. You haven't lost yet. Go ask your father."

XXIV

"You think Alan really meant it when he said he'd given up?" asked Billy, turning down the flame under the frying pan. He was cooking a toasted-cheese-and-worm sandwich.

"I don't know," said Tom, looking in the refrigerator. "I suppose so. He asked us to the Mets game —Say, is that chocolate pudding?"

"Yeah, but don't take any. It's for supper."

"I could just scrape some off the top, and then you could tell your mother it fell out upside down on the floor by mistake while you were getting the cheese out, so you scraped the dirty part off into the garbage."

"Welllll—" said Billy doubtfully.

"Thomas Grout," said Billy's mother, coming in from the hall. "I'm surprised at you."

The Twelfth Worm

"Aw, Mrs. Forrester, I wouldn't really have done it. I was just, you know, *talking*. Everybody talks: my father, Billy's father, Billy, my sisters Annie, Charlotte, Polly—" He was backing toward the door. "—Betty, Agnes, Columbus—"

"I didn't know you had a sister named Columbus, Tom," said Billy's mother. "Would you like some chocolate ice cream instead?"

"Oh, sure, Mrs. Forrester," said Tom, relieved. He sat down at the table. "It's my cousin who's named Columbus." He grinned. "Columbus Ohio. He's a capital fellow, Mrs. Forrester."

And then he had to grab the edge of the table to keep from rolling off his chair laughing at his own joke. Billy looked disgusted. His mother opened the refrigerator, shaking her head.

XXV

Pearl Harbor

THE car slid quietly to a stop under the streetlight outside Billy's house.

"Shhh," whispered Alan to his father. "Billy's asleep."

His father glanced back at Billy, snoring peacefully in the back seat, his plump cheeks sticky with orange soda.

"Alan, run up to the house and tell them I'm bringing Billy in."

Billy's father met them at the front door, and taking Billy, whispered his thanks. Alan and his father went down the walk. Behind them the porch light clicked off.

In the back seat of the car Joe and Alan wrestled gleefully.

"We did it!" "We've won!" "He'll never wake up now!"

Alan struggled out of Joe's grip and asked his father what time it was.

"Late. Almost midnight, I think."

Joe pulled Alan's head down and tried to sit on it.

"He couldn't do it now even if he woke up. How could he find and cook and eat a worm in the *dark?* Hee, hee. We've won! We've won!"

XXVI

Guadalcanal

BUT slumped on the bathroom stool, his mother holding up his chin while she washed his face, Billy was waking.

"Hold still, dear. Did you have a good time? You're certainly home late. Is this part of winning the bet?"

Billy's eyes blinked sleepily. He had a gnawing feeling he had forgotten something. He hiccupped, gazing dopily down at the fuzzy blue bathmat . . . yawned . . . He'd remember in the morning. It couldn't be that im—

BET!?!

BET!?!

He hadn't won yet! There were still three to go! Fifteen! Fifteen worms in fifteen days! Today was . . .

He jumped up.

"Mom, I haven't eaten my worm today!"

And suddenly it all came to him. The whole trip . . . all the candy bars, hot dogs, hamburgers, popcorn.

"What time is it, Mom? Quick!"

"About quarter to twelve."

"It was a *trick!*" He snatched his pants off the

floor. "They were trying to make me forget!" He tumbled and slid downstairs, through the dining room, his shirttail flying, yanked open the drawer in the kitchen table, snatched out the flashlight, the drawer spilling out with a clatter and crash onto the floor, and slammed out the back door.

"The finks!"

He scuttled across the back field toward Tom's house, searching the ground with the flashlight as he went.

"There! Darn, a stick! Geez, suppose I can't find one?"

He stopped.

"There won't be time to cook it!"

He ran on.

"And no ketchup."

He stopped.

"I'll bet Tom wasn't sick at all."

He ran on. The night was moonless and close. He paused to heave over a rotten log in the high, dewy grass—mealybugs and scooters—clambered over the stone wall into Tom's backyard . . . and was all of a sudden wrestling with a pup tent.

Muffled grunts and thrashings.

"Tom!" he yelled. "Tom! It's me! Billy! They're trying to trick us."

Tom and his younger brother Pete crawled out from under the pup tent.

"It was a trick," panted Billy. "Alan and Joe were trying to make me forget. Fifteen worms in fif-

teen days. If I don't eat one in the next ten minutes, Alan'll say he's won. It's almost midnight."

"And they left me home so I wouldn't remind you?"

Billy nodded.

"Have you got a worm?"

"We'll have to find one."

Tom dug back into the pup tent and came up with two flashlights. They zigzagged back and forth across the lawn, bent over, searching.

"I got one!" cried Pete.

"Shhh."

"I'll have to eat it raw," said Billy. He threw back his head.

"Wait," whispered Tom, grabbing his arm. "You should do it where Alan and Joe can see you. Pete, run and get your siren out of the garage."

XXVII

U<small>NDER</small> the streetlight in front of Alan's house Tom and Pete knelt over the siren. Billy stood beside them, the night crawler squirming in his fingers.

"Now wait till lots of lights come on all over, in all the houses," said Tom. "Then chomp it down. Ready, Pete? Now."

The siren growled, winding slowly up and up until it

SCREEEEEEEEEEEEEEEEEEEEEEEECHED! across the sleeping neighborhood, sending birds squawking and chirping into the air from trees and rooftops; dogs began to bark; windows lit up; there were confused shouts, bangs of windows slamming up.

"Ladies and gentlemen," shouted Tom through the dying whine of the siren, "Alan Phelps and Jo-

The Thirteenth Worm

seph O'Hara, through their finkiness and cheating, their lies and dirty—"

"Come *on*," muttered Billy, his head thrown back, dangling the worm over his open mouth. "We haven't got much time."

"Alan Phelps and Joseph O'Hara," shouted Tom, "have forced us to wake you all up so that you may now witness, ta-ratta-ta-ratta-ta-ratta-ta-ta: THE EATING OF THE THIRTEENTH WORM!"

He dropped to his knees; the siren wound slowly up to a SCREECH! Billy dropped the crawler into his mouth and chewed furiously, his eyes closed; fell to his knees, still chewing, his face turning beet-red; toppled over on his side, still chewing; rolled and writhed about the sidewalk, clutching his stomach, still chewing—Tom and Pete kneeling by the street-light, working the screaming siren. . . .

Billy threw open his arms and lay still on his back under the glare of the streetlight, his mouth wide open.

"TAAA—RAAAAAAAAaaaaaaaaaaaa!" announced Tom, springing up and pointing to Billy.

The three boys ran off into the darkness. As they went, Tom yelled, "Remember: Alan Phelps and Joseph O'Hara."

XXVIII

A confused murmur arose up and down the street. Suddenly a boy shouted from the Phelps's house.

"Finks!"

Alan's father dragged him back from the window.

"Is that why you were stuffing Billy with candy and junk all day?"

"Leave me alone. Yeah. We were trying to trick him. The fink. FINKS!" he yelled at the top of his voice, lunging toward the window.

"Quiet!"

His father sat him down hard in a chair.

Joe peered furtively out through the fringe of the bedspread. As soon as he had heard the siren and Tom's yells, he had crawled under the bed.

"And that's why Billy woke the whole neighborhood up? to show you he hadn't been tricked?"

"Yes."

His father let go of Alan's pajama collar. In the doorway Alan's mother threw up her hands and went off to the bathroom to take two aspirin.

The next day Alan and Joe tramped from house

Hello, We're . . . .

to house in the neighborhood, knocking on each door and then reciting in chorus:

"Hello. We're Alan Phelps and Joseph O'Hara. We're the reason you were waked up in the middle of the night last night, and we're sorry." Breath. "You'll be happy to know our parents have punished us we can't look at television or have any dessert for a month and our allowances have been taken away for two weeks we promise that it will never happen again."

"At least not in *this* neighborhood," muttered Joe as the last door closed behind them.

"And Alan," said his father at dinner that night, "I don't want to hear that there has been any repetition of this incident at Billy's or Tom's house or anywhere else. Do you understand that?"

"But we can't let them get away with it, Mr. Phelps," called Joe from the living room, where he was waiting for Alan to finish dinner.

"There will be *no* repetition of this incident or anything like it," repeated Mr. Phelps. "You tried to trick Billy and lost. That will be the end of the matter."

XXIX

Y ou know what you are?" said Alan, his nose almost touching Billy's. "You're a *bastard.*"

"And you're *another,*" sneered Billy through clenched teeth. "And a cheating, lying, dirty, snot-nosed, cheating, *lying* one."

"If you say *two more words,*" said Alan, "you know what? I'll beat your head in."

Billy breathed hard.

"I'm right behind you," muttered Tom, peering grimly over Billy's shoulder, his fists clenched.

"Yeah?" said Joe from behind Alan. "So what? We can lick both of you with our hands tied behind our backs and paper bags over our heads."

"You couldn't lick a *flea.*"

"Yeah?"

"Yeah."

Spiffle!

Whack!

Thump!

"Someone's choking! No fair!"

Thwomp!

Gouge!

Joe crawled off behind a tree, nose bleeding.

Womp!

"He's pulling hair!"
"He's scratching!"

Twist!
Tsiwt!

Alan crawled weeping behind a bush.

Thump!   Whack!   Donk!

"Billy! It's just you and me!"

"Where're the others?"

Tom and Billy untangled and sat up, bruised, scratched, dusty, shirts torn, hair tousled. Tom's nose was bleeding, Billy's shoe had come off.

"Yaaaaaaa ya!" sassed Alan and Joe from behind the tree.

Billy started to shake his fist at them and clamber up, but then sank back. Tom panted beside him, bleary-eyed.

"Yaaaaaaa ya, all worn out? Can't fight anymore?"

Alan scooped up a handful of mud and flung it at Tom and Billy. Then Joe did the same. Billy and

Tom scrambled up and pelted back. Mud splattered
against trees and bushes. Alan began to cry. A rock
hit Billy over the eye. He sat down backward in the
mud, covering his head with his arms, sobbing. Joe
and Tom stopped throwing. Joe grabbed Alan.
"Come on."

Tom knelt beside Billy. "Lemme see, Billy. Is it
bad? Take your arms away so I can see." He tried to
pull Billy's arms apart. Billy wrenched away.

"Come on," said Tom in a scared voice. "I'll take
you home. Come on. Your mother can take you to
the doctor."

ALAN and Joe sat on the sofa, Tom and Billy on two straight chairs opposite them.

"Now," said Alan's father. "What's this all about?"

The four boys all began talking at once, accusing, recounting, explaining.

"All right," said Alan's father after a while. "That's enough. Now we know it's got something to do with this bet Alan and Billy made, but Mr. O'Hara and I aren't going to get involved in that. You'll have to settle that among yourselves."

"You four boys have been friends too long to start fighting now," said Mr. O'Hara. "You really hurt each other. Look at yourselves, your faces all bruised and muddy. Talk it over, work things out, and then you can shake and be friends again."

Joe muttered under his breath, "I couldn't be friends with those rats."

"We'll be out in the kitchen," said Alan's father. "When you've settled it, call us, and we'll all go down to Friendly's for some ice cream. Okay?"

Billy and Alan and Tom nodded. The two fathers left the room. The boys gazed silently at each other. After a while, Alan said, "It wasn't us that scratched Tom. Billy did it."

Another silence.

The Peace Treaty

"Did you have stitches?" Billy asked Alan.

"Naw. Did you?"

Billy shook his head.

More silence.

"You tried to cheat," said Billy.

"That wasn't cheating. We were just trying to trick you."

"Yeah, but before that. When you glued the two worms together. That was cheating."

"You would have cheated, too, if you'd been losing."

Billy thought about it.

"Okay. But look, no *more* cheating. I've already eaten thirteen worms; you know I can eat two more. Heck, if I buy George Cunningham's brother's minibike, we can all use it—we'll all have fun with it."

Joe and Alan glanced at each other.

"Okay," said Joe. "You win. He wins, Alan."

"Yeah, but—"

"What's the use?" said Joe. "We've tried everything. I'm sick of it. Geez, we've done nothing else for almost two weeks."

Alan scratched his eyebrow, glancing at Joe. "Yeah, but—"

Joe stood up. "Come on. At least we'll get a milk shake out of it."

BILLY lifted the worm out of the frying pan with the cooking tongs and curled it back and forth on his peanut-butter sandwich.

"I bet they try something," he said. "Joe won't give up. Alan might, but Joe won't."

Tom was carving his initials in the leg of the kitchen table. "Yeah, but it's not Joe's bet. What does he care?"

"Just the same I bet he tries something."

Billy sat down at the table, turning the sandwich this way and that, looking for the best spot to take the first bite.

Emily came in from the dining room.

"You and mom got a letter."

Chewing, Billy opened it.

The Letter

Charles M. McGrath, M.D.
34 Beechwood Drive
Gratton, New York 12601

Midnight, August 15, 1923

Mrs. John Forrester
7 Manchester Road
East Gratton, N. Y. 12603

Dear Mrs. Forrester:

    I have just made a distressing
discovery. ~~As whit lubingtingh while~~ *leafing through*
a medical journal before going up to
bed, I noticed an article entittled
"Poisons in the Home Garden", a sub-
ject which neccessarily fascinates.
me. As I glanced through the article
a phase c aught my eye: "Lumbricus
terrestris, the common earthw orm."
I read on.
    Mrs. Forrester, let me assurre
you, first of all, that th ere is no
cause for undue alarm. However, you
will, I am sure, be concerned to learn
that "especially in the months of July
and August parents must beware of the

99

common earthworm, some varieties of
which are known to secrete a substance
(Lumbricus coreopsis), which, though
not malignant to the skin, is sometimes harmful if swallowed. Dr. A.
C. Roosevelt of Hyde Park, New York,
reports that 10% of the boys studied
report ed no ill effects except in-
duced paralysis of the lower fulmar
region; 40% reported abdominal cramp-
ing, triple vision (lasting from two
to thr ee years and impairing school
performance) and extreme lussitude;
autopsy repobts have not yet been
recieved on the remaining 50%, and so
no final conclusions canbe drawn, but
 extreme caution is urged since the
blackened and pimply faces of the
subjects lead one to suspect the
worse."
       Mrs. Forrester, as your friànd
and family phisician, I would strong-
ly recommend that your son William
eat no mere worms until I return on
Thursday from New York City and ca n
give him a thurough examination.

            Yours sincerely,

            C, M. McGrath, M.D.

CMM/ac

XXXII

Croak

His hand trembling, Billy laid the peanut-butter-and-fried-worm sandwich down on the table.

"Do you think—"

"Wow," whispered Tom.

The screen door banged.

Billy's father came into the kitchen, his tie loosened, his jacket over his arm. He laid his briefcase on the table.

"It's hot," he said cheerfully.

Billy staggered to the sink and feebly drew himself a glass of water.

Tom and Emily watched him, awestruck.

"What's the matter?" asked Billy's father.

Water dribbled down Billy's chin and onto his T-shirt as he drank. His mind swam. Poison? Paralysis? Extreme lassitude?

"*Tom,*" said Billy's father, "what's going on?"

Tom pointed at the letter lying on the table.

Billy's father read it, smiled, glanced at Billy, and getting a beer out of the refrigerator, sat down at the table.

"Well," he said to Billy. "So it fooled you, eh?"

"Fooled me?" croaked Billy.

XXXIII
The Fourteenth Worm

BUT how could Alan and Joe know all those medical words, Mr. Forrester?" said Tom. "Lumbricus coreopsis? Fulmar?"

"Do you know what fulmar really means?"

Tom and Billy shook their heads.

"It means a bird, a seabird, I think."

"Boy," said Billy, disgusted. He sat back down at the table and picked up his sandwich.

"They could be arrested, Mr. Forrester," said Tom. "Couldn't they be arrested for defrauding the mails? Couldn't they?"

Billy grinned and bit down on the peanut-butter-and-fried-worm sandwich.

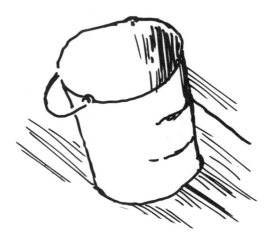

XXXIV

The Fifteenth....

STANDING on a rusty pail, Billy peered through a crack into the horse barn. Joe was wandering about lashing at cobwebs with a stick; Alan was slumped on a barrel, gnawing his thumbnail.

Billy went around to the door.

"Hi," he said.

Alan didn't look up.

"Hi," said Joe.

Billy glanced around suspiciously.

"Take it easy," said Joe. "We concede. At least I do. *He's* still trying to think up something." He pointed at Alan with the stick.

"Where's Tom?" said Billy.

"He wouldn't eat his lunch, so his mother kept him in."

Billy leaned over the platter on the orange crate and smelled the steaming, Southern-fried worm.

"He wanted to load it with red pepper," said Joe, "but I wouldn't let him."

Billy forked ketchup, mustard, and piccalilli onto the platter, cut a piece of worm, dipped it in the glop, stuck it in his mouth, chewed nervously . . . swallowed . . . cut another piece. . . . The worm tasted better than usual, sort of like kidney beans, Southern-fried kidney beans.

"Where'd you get this one?"

"Down behind Bannerman's," said Joe.

"From the *muck!*" yelled Alan. "The *muck!* Gooey, slimy, stagnant *muck!*"

Billy grinned. "Yeah? You'll have to show me. This is the best one yet."

Alan jumped up and kicked the barrel clattering into a stall. Joe shrugged at Billy, grinning. Billy held up the last bite.

"Ta-rahhhh."

He swallowed it.

"Okay, lemme look," said Alan. "Come on." He peered into Billy's mouth.

"Oh, no. Come on. There's some still stuck between your teeth there."

Billy sucked noisily at his teeth.

"Okay?"

Alan's shoulders slumped.

"I can't get the money till tomorrow," he said. "Oh, geez. You know I'll have to work Saturdays for six *months* to pay it back."

He trudged slowly toward the door.

"Comin', Joe?"

"Yeah, maybe your father won't act so bad if I'm there when you tell him."

Alan stopped in the door.

"Tomorrow?" he said without turning. "Ten o'clock?"

He sounded as if he was going to cry.

"Yeah, sure," said Billy. "Make it later if you want."

"Naw. It's not going to do any good putting it off. Come on, Joe."

XXXV

Burp

LEFT alone in the barn, Billy hugged himself.

"I won! I won! Fifty dollars. Ha, ha."

He sat down on the crate, grinning.

"Heck, *I* knew I could do it. Ha. I was so scared at first, waking everybody up in the middle of the night."

He burped—beans.

"I should have made it *thirty* worms and *one hundred* dollars. That stupid letter. Joe knew when he was licked though. Ha. Gcez."

BEANS?!!?

He stood up.

How come that burp had tasted like beans? He'd had a hamburger for lunch. And a glass of milk. Then the worm. Say . . . they couldn't have. . . ?

He snatched up the platter. Nothing left, just a few crumbs of cornmeal. Craning his neck, his eyes bugging out, straining, he . . . he . . . *burped:* beans!

Again: *beans!*

He burst out of the barn, stumbling over the sill, yelling. Across the field Joe and Alan turned. Alan started to run; Joe grabbed his arm.

"It was a *fake!*" panted Billy, coming up to them. "You *faked* it! It wasn't a real worm!"

105

"Real worm?" said Joe. "What're you talking about?"

"You *made* a worm!" yelled Billy. "Out of beans! Then tomorrow you were going to say I'd lost, I hadn't eaten fifteen worms—the last one was *fake.*"

"Oh, geez," said Alan. "Come *on,* will ya?"

"He didn't do it while I was around," said Joe. "You sure? What'd you have for lunch?"

"A hamburger and milk."

"Yeah, but where'd you get the hamburger?"

"I don't know. My mother bought it. What difference does that make?"

"Yeah, well, a lot of the hamburg you get these days has stuff mixed in it. You know, sausage meat, soybeans, bread crumbs. So the butcher makes more money."

"Yeah, yeah, yeah," said Billy. "Sure. But anyway, you come on back. Just to make sure, I'm going to eat *another* worm."

"Geez, suit yourself. Eat *four* more. Come on, Alan, let's go. Let him eat what he wants."

XXXVI

The Fifteenth Wo. . . .

BILLY threw back his head, lowered the worm
. . . Alan *charged* around the door! *leaped* on Billy's back! *flung him* to the ground! punching! yelling! . . . jumped up! grabbed Billy's feet! dragged
him bump-bump-bump across the rough chaffy floor
to the tool closet! bundled him inside! slammed the
door! *locked* it!

Silence. Water trickling into the trough outside,
Alan panting. . . .

"What're you gonna do with him?" Joe asked
hoarscly from the doorway.

"IF HE'S IN THE CLOSET, HE CAN'T EAT
THE WORM, CAN HE?"

"You're crazy. He'll start to yell. His parents'll
hear him."

"YEAH? YEAH?"

Alan's hair was mussed; his shirttail hung out.

"Yeah," said Joe, eyeing him. "He will. He'll
start to yell and his parents'll hear him."

Alan glanced wildly about . . . started toward
the door . . . turned. . . .

"Not if we put him down the cistern."

"The *cistern?*" Joe wiped his mouth. "Alan, cut
it out. It's only fifty dollars. Come on. Face it.

You've lost. You can't put Billy down in that cistern all by himself. Suppose there's water in it? It's fifteen feet deep."

"We can lower him down with a rope."

BANG! BANG! BANG! BANG! BANG!

Billy was kicking the tool-closet door.

"LEMME OUT! HELP! LEMME OUT! IT'S CHEATING! HELP! I wanna get out, I wanna get out, I wanna get out—"

BANG! BANG! BANG! BANG!

He chanted rhythmically, kicking the door with both feet in time with his chant.

Alan ran across the barn and grabbing hold of a beam, skidding to a stop, began to kick aside the hay and trash which littered the planks over the old cistern.

BANG! BANG! BANG! BANG!

"I wanna get out, I wanna get out, I wanna get out—"

"Come on!" Alan yelled at Joe. "Help me! We were all down in it last year. How's it gonna hurt him? Come on. It'll work. I'll split with you. Get some rope."

BANG! BANG! BANG! BANG!

"I wanna get out, I—"

XXXVII

Out of the Frying Pan into the Oven

On his knees, yanking at the planks which covered the old cistern, thinking, I've got him. I've got him. I win. He'll never . . . Alan felt a hand grip his shoulder, glanced up. . . .

"WHAT THE DEVIL IS GOING ON IN HERE?" Mr. Forrester shouted down at him.

BANG! BANG! BANG! BANG!

"I wanna—"

A confused babble of voices, dying out suddenly.

"Now," said Mr. Forrester. "Alan and Joe: *home!* Scoot."

Alan and Joe crowded out the door.

"I've *won!*" crowed Billy. He danced toward the platter. "Nothing can—"

"Billy! Up to your room!"

"I just got to eat this worm, Dad. Ho, ho, I've won! I've won!"

"BILLY! Up to your ROOM!"

"Dad, I—"

His father pointed.

109

"Dad, if I don't eat what's left, I'll lose; Alan'll win. It's just two—"

"*Now.* The bet is over. You know what I've told you about that cistern. NOW!"

"Dad, I'll *lose!* I'll *lose!* Alan'll—"

"Then you will learn something. *March!*"

"You mean I can't even eat *that last little bit?* How long could it take me? What could—"

"*Billy. Now.*"

XXXVIII

$ % // ! ? Blip */ & !

BILLY kicked the bed.

He'd *won*. All hc'd had tu du was eat two more bites, *two bites*.

He kicked the wall.

What'd his father gotten so mad for? *Alan* had started opening the cistern, not him.

Geez, he hadn't even let him *explain*. Twice. Twice he'd won and then something had happened.

And now he was going to lose? After all he'd gone through? Nightmares, fights, thinking he'd been poisoned? All for nothing?

He kicked the bed.

XXXIX

The United States Cavalry Rides over the Hilltop

MRS. FORRESTER?" said Tom, peering through the screen door. "Could I see Billy for a minute?"

"He's up in his room being punished, Tom. He and Joe and Alan were very naughty this afternoon."

"Yeah?" said Tom. "No kidding? What'd they do?"

XL

The Fifteenth Worm

BILLY kicked the wall again.

Two minutes. What difference could *two minutes* have made?

He leaned his forehead against the windowpane, gazing dejectedly out into the backyard.

That's what always happened—somebody . . .

Tom's younger brother Pete appeared suddenly around the corner of the house, running, holding up a little yellow Easter basket . . . gesturing?

THE WORM! TOM! Pete had brought him a worm! The fifteenth worm!

Billy slammed up the window.

"Catch!" yelled Pete.

"Hurry!
Tom's talking
to your
mother!"

He heaved a brick with a string tied to it up to Billy; Billy caught it, hauled the string up hand over hand, the basket came bobbing up the side of the house. Alan and Joe plunged out of the bushes. . . . Billy snatched the tin can out of the Easter basket, plucked out a huge, squirming night crawler . . .

"MRS. FORRESTER! MRS. FORRESTER!"

Alan and Joe shouted at the top of their lungs, dancing about on the lawn, waving their arms.

"MRS. FORRESTER! MRS. FORRESTER!"

"TOO LATE!" yelled Billy gleefully.

Throwing back his head, he dropped the squirming night crawler into his mouth . . . chewed and chewed. Tom and Mrs. Forrester appeared around the corner of the house.

"Too glate!" Billy yelled, still chewing. "Too glate! I gwin!"

He disappeared from the window . . . a door slammed inside the house, a trampling on the stairs . . . he burst out the kitchen door . . . a flying leap off the back steps. He rolled, scrambled up, yelling, "I win! I win! I win!" grabbed Tom's hands. They danced round and round and round, Pete cavorting beside them.

Joe and Alan slunk off through the bushes.

. . . round and round and round . . .

Billy's mother laughed and went into the kitchen.

. . . round and round and round . . . till they collapsed on their backs in the grass.

"I win," gasped Billy to the blue, cloudless sky. "I *win*."

XLI
Epilogue

BILLY leaned the minibike against a tree and started down the path through the woods. Tom and Joe were already sitting by a smoldering trash fire on the riverbank, opening their lunch bags.

"Where's Alan? At the store?" asked Billy, flopping down by Tom.

"Yeah," said Joe. "He's still got two weeks to go."

"What have you got for lunch?" asked Tom.

Billy looked embarrassed.

"Worm-and-egg on rye."

"Heck," said Tom. "Why can't you ever bring something somebody else likes, so you can trade?"

Billy frowned. He opened his lunch bag.

"I don't know. I just can't stop. I don't dare tell my mother. I even like the *taste* now." He scratched his head. "Do you think there's something the doctors don't know? Do you think I could be the first person who's ever been *hooked* on worms?"